T0149382

PRAYER POWER:

BREAKING THE CYCLE OF FAILURE

Bright Osigwe

New Heart Assembly Ministries
Houston, Texas, U.S.A.
www.newheartassembly.org

authorHOUSE

AuthorHouse™
1663 Liberty Drive
Bloomington, IN 47403
www.authorhouse.com
Phone: 1 (800) 839-8640

Published by AuthorHouse 02/13/2020

ISBN: 978-1-5462-6891-8 (sc)
ISBN: 978-1-5462-6890-1 (e)

Print information available on the last page.

Cover art and design: Bright Osigwe

This book is printed on acid-free paper.

For more information or to order additional copies, please contact:
Bright Osigwe
brightosigwe@sbcglobal.net

Preface

"This Book of the Law shall not depart from your mouth; but you shall meditate in it day and night, that you may observe to do according to all that is written in it. For then you will make your way prosperous, and then you will have good success," (Joshua 1:8).

You need to pray these powerful words found in God's instructions to Joshua with your mouth (Talking), believe them with your heart (Meditate), and observe to do them (Try out). This is God's recipe for success for all His children. If you want true and lasting success, you can't have better advice. And it is so simple: Talk, Think and Try Out the Word of God, on a daily basis. Then watch your measure of faith grow, and grow, and grow ...; you'll see your mountains moved away; you'll receive many miracles and experience greater prayer power. Without faith you cannot please God (Heb. 11:6), or demonstrate the enemy's defeat (1 Jn.5:4). And true faith comes by hearing the Word of God (Rom. 10:17) and the Holy Spirit (Zech. 4:6).

Prayer Power is a self-help kit designed to help you develop a solid, biblical kind of prayer life that pleases God and gets results. This book could transform your prayer life, and affect the lives of your loved ones and friends.

So dear child of God, arise and shine, take your rightful place in God's program and possess your possessions (Obad. 17). Amen!

Dedication

I dedicate this book to my mother, Cyrina Osigwe, a follower of our Lord and Savior Jesus Christ, talented, intelligent, who had what it took to raise her children, more than a conqueror, an overcome, and greatly favored by God. Thanks for being an awesome mother.

I DECLARE

"'*No weapon forged against you will prevail, and you will refute every tongue that accuses you. This is the heritage of the servants of the Lord, and this is their vindication for me,' declares the LORD*" (Isaiah 54:17).

"*The Lord will rescue me from every evil attack and will bring me safely to his heavenly kingdom. To him be glory for ever and ever. Amen*" (2 Timothy 4:18).

SECURITY

Confess three times daily:

> A thousand may fall at my side and ten thousand at my right hand, but it shall not come near me!

I declare that God watches over me and protects me from all evil. No evil shall befall me, and no plague shall come near my dwelling. Because the Greater One lives in me, He preserves me, and the wicked one does not touch me. A thousand may fall at my side and ten thousand at my right hand, but it shall not come near me. So I am safe from all witches, wizards, thieves, armed robbers, evil spirits, and all forces of darkness (Psalm 91).

I declare that the blood of Jesus covers me and their arrows return to sender. I am never alone, God is with me and He is for me. His angels fight for me, and supply my every need. I laugh at the devil for he is a liar, and a loser. I am not moved at all by what I see, or what I feel, I am moved only by the Word that is real, the Word of God. On Christ the Solid Rock I stand, all other ground is sinking sand.

Some boast of chariots and horses, but I boast in the Lord my God. Without God, the watchmen watch in vain and the builders build in vain. But the Lord watches over me, today and every day. I am His beloved, and He gives me good sleep. I succeed in everything, for Jesus gives me the victory. Hallelujah, Amen.

BIBLE REFERENCES for meditations:

Ps 91; 1 Jn. 4:4, 5:8; Isa. 54:17; Rev. 12:11; Matt. 28:20; Ps. 35:5-6; Job 5:22; 2 Cor. 5:7; Ps. 20:7; Ps. 127; Jn. 16:32

I DECLARE

I declare that I will serve the Lord my God, and He will bless my bread and my water. And God will take sickness away from my midst. No one shall suffer miscarriage or be barren in my land; I will fulfill the number of my days (Exodus 23:25, 26).

I declare that God Himself took my infirmities and bore my sicknesses (Matthew 8:17).

DIVINE HEALTH

Confess three times daily:

I declare that I will bless the Lord O my soul, and forget none of His benefits. He forgives my sins and heals all my diseases. He delivers my life from premature death, and crowns me with loving kindness and tender mercies. He satisfies my mouth with good things, so that I stay young and healthy like an eagle. God wishes above all things that I should prosper and be in health even as my soul prospers.

> I declare that I will bless the Lord O my soul, and forget none of His benefits.

I declare that God blesses everything I eat and drink and takes away sickness from around me. There is no kind of barrenness or miscarriage in my life. The number of my days shall be fulfilled. Amen. The same Spirit that raised Christ from the dead dwells in me and quickens my mortal body. He gives Resurrection Life to every part of my body, Amen.

I declare that Jesus took my infirmities, and carried my sicknesses and diseases. By His stripes I have been healed. The anointing has broken the yoke. He has sent His Word and healed me and has delivered me from all destructions. There shall no evil befall me neither shall any plague come near my dwelling. He is *Jehovah-Rapha*, the Lord that heals me. Death and life are in the power of my tongue, so I always speak life and not death to my body.

I declare and confess my body is strong and healthy. I speak to every cell in my body, every organ, every tissue, muscle, fiber, nerve, blood vessel. Be strong and function perfectly, as God made you to function, in Jesus' name. Amen.

I declare my body is the temple of the Holy Spirit; it must not be defiled by sickness. Therefore, every disease, germ and virus, that touches my body, dies instantly in the name of Jesus.

I declare and command **All** demons and spirits of infirmity, return to sender, in Jesus' name, Amen. I can do all things through Christ who strengthens me. By faith I am doing what I could not do before. I confess healing for my body in Jesus' name, Amen. Thank you, Lord, for healing me. Amen.

BIBLE REFERENCES for meditation:

Ps. 103:1-5; 3 Jn. 2; Ex. 23:25, 26; Rom. 8.11; Matt. 8:17; 1 Pt. 2:24; Isa. 10:27; Ps. 91:10, 107:20; Ex. 15:24; Prov. 18:21; 1 Cor. 6:19; Ps. 35:8; Phil. 4:13

I DECLARE

"In their hearts humans plan their course, but the LORD establishes their steps" (Proverbs 16:9).

"If any of you lacks wisdom, let him ask of God, who gives to all liberally and without reproach, and it will be given him" (James 1:5). I declare that I have all the wisdom I need to succeed in life, in Jesus' name, Amen.

DIVINE GUIDANCE

Confess three times daily:

The Spirit of Truth abides in me and teaches me all things. Therefore, I confess I have perfect knowledge of every situation and circumstance that I come up against, for I am filled with the knowledge of His will, in all wisdom and spiritual understanding.

I declare that I will commit my works unto the Lord so my plans are established. I trust the Lord with all my heart and I lean not unto my own understanding, in all my ways I acknowledge Him and He directs my paths. There is a way that seems right unto men, but it leads to destruction. Therefore, I do not follow the advice of the ungodly, nor stand in the way of sinners, nor sit with mockers. But I delight in the Word of God. I meditate on it day and night.

I declare that I will never worry about anything, instead, I pray about everything and the peace of God which passes all understanding guards my heart and mind in Christ Jesus. By the help of the Spirit, I always pray right, and I receive answers to my petitions.

> I declare that I will commit my works unto the Lord so my plans are established.

I declare and decree that God guides me by my human spirit, which is the candle of the Lord. He reveals His will to me through the Bible, and through anointed sermons, prophecies, tongues and interpretations, visions and revelations, and still, small voices within. And by the mouth of 2 or 3 independent witnesses, every word is established. Because I am led by the Spirit of God today, I will never go astray. I am never confused, or double-minded. For the Lord is my shepherd; I know His voice, and the voice of the stranger, I never follow. I shall hear His voice behind me saying, "This is the way, walk in it," whether I go to the right or to the left. The Lord guides me by His counsel, and makes my way perfect. Amen.

BIBLE REFERENCES for meditation:

Ps. 1:1-4, 23:1-2; Prov. 3:5-6, 16:9; Matt. 6:25, 30; Luke 12:25; John 14:17; Rom. 8:24; Phil. 4:7; Jms. 1:7-8; Jude 20

I DECLARE

I declare that I will honor the Lord with my possessions, and with the first fruits of all my increase, so my barns will be filled with plenty (Proverbs 3:9, 10).

I declare that my God shall supply all my needs according to His riches in glory by Christ Jesus.

PROSPERITY

Confess three times daily:

I confess that the Lord is my shepherd, I shall never lack. He supplies my needs according to His riches and by His power. Christ has redeemed me from the curse of the law. For poverty, He has given me wealth, for sickness, He has given me health, for death, He has given me eternal life. I declare that Abraham's blessings are mine; I am blessed in the morning; I am blessed in the evening; I am blessed going out, and I am blessed coming in. I am blessed today and every day of my life. I am the head and not the tail; I am the first and not the last. I am above only, never beneath.

I declare that Abraham's blessings are mine; I am blessed in the morning; I am blessed in the evening; I am blessed going out, and I am blessed coming in.

I declare God is a giver, so I am a giver. I give and it is given unto me, good measure, pressed down, shaken together, and running over, men give unto my bosom. It is more blessed to give than to receive. God loves a cheerful giver. He multiplies my seeds that are my gifts and sacrifices, and gives me power to get wealth. The more I give, the more I receive, and God supplies me with all good things so that in all things and at all times I have all I need, so I can give again. I do good to all, to widows and orphans, to my friends and even enemies; I do good especially to the children of God.

I declare that the Lord has opened the windows of heaven, and has poured down the blessings, not a trickle, not a stream, but a flood. I am in the flood stage of blessings: God has rebuked the devourer for my sake. Therefore, Satan, take your hands off all my money. Let the angels of God go and bring them in. In Jesus' name, I command these items to come to me (**specify them**). I believe I have received. Jesus is my provider and He is Lord of all, Amen.

BIBLE REFERENCES for meditation:

Ps. 23:1; Phil. 4:19; Gal. 3:13-14; Dt. 28:1-14; Lk. 6:38; Acts 20:35; 2 Cor. 9:6-15; Deut. 8:18; Prov. 11:24-26; Ps. 84:11; Jms. 1:27; Gal. 6:9-10; Mal. 3:8-12; Mt. 18:18; Job 22:28; Gen. 11:14

I DECLARE

"*I have hidden your word in my heart that I might not sin against you.*" (Psalm 119:11).

"*In the same way, count yourselves dead to sin but alive to God in Christ Jesus. Therefore, do not let sin reign in your mortal body so that you obey its evil desires. Do not offer any part of yourself to sin as an instrument of wickedness, but rather offer yourselves to God as those who have been brought from death to life; and offer every part of yourself to Him as an instrument of righteousness.....For sin shall no longer be your master...*" (Romans 6:11-14).

A HOLY LIFE

Confess three times daily:

I declare I'm a holy child of a holy God. I walk in the Spirit, so I do not fulfill the lusts of the flesh. Denying all ungodliness and worldly lusts, I live soberly, righteously and godly, in this present world, while I await the glorious appearing of the Lord Jesus Christ. This is my Blessed Hope.

FAITH THAT MOVES MOUNTAIN

I declare that with God nothing shall be impossible for me (Luke 1:37).

Heavenly Father I strongly believe that with you nothing shall be impossible because I believe. My God will never forget me. It is written, "*Can a mother forget the baby at her breast and have no compassion on child she has borne? Though she may forget, I will not forget you!*" (Isaiah 49:15). Heavenly Father, I know you cannot forget me for I am the works of thine hand. Answer my prayers and let my joy be full in Jesus' name. Amen.

> I walk in the Spirit, so I do not fulfill the lusts of the flesh.

It is written, "*This is what the Sovereign LORD says to these bones: I will make breath enter you, and you will come to life*" (Ezekiel 37:5). I declare, Heavenly Father, cause new life to come into me, my business and all that belongs to me. I command every organ in me to be functioning fine, in Jesus' name, Amen.

8

It is written, "*And I will do whatever you ask in my name, so that the Father may be glorified in the Son*" (John 14:13). I declare and confess Lord Jesus do all that I will ask you now so that the Father may be glorified in you the Son, Amen.

It is written, "*God blessed them and said to them, 'Be fruitful and increase in number: fill the earth and subdue it. Rule over the fish of the sea and the birds of the sky and over any living creature that moves on the ground'*" (Genesis 1:28). I declare and confess Heavenly Father cause me to be fruitful and multiply and to replenish the earth and subdue it. I claim dominion in Jesus' name.

I declare Heavenly Father command all your blessings to come upon me and prosper all the works of my hand. Anything I shall lay my hand upon me and prosper all the works of my hand. Anything I shall lay my hand upon from today shall prosper in Jesus' name, Amen.

It is written, "*The LORD will open the heavens, the storehouse of his bounty, to send rain on your land in season and to bless all the work of your hands. You will lend to many nations but will borrow from none*" (Deuteronomy 28:12). I declare Heavenly Father open unto me Your good treasure and give me the former and latter rain of blessings. Bless all the works of my hand so that I will lend to many nations. I refuse to lack and I refuse to borrow or beg all the days of my life in Jesus' name, Amen.

It is written, "*The LORD will make you the head, not the tail. If you pay attention to the commands of the LORD your God that I give you this day and carefully follow them, you will always be at the top, never at the bottom*" (Deuteronomy 28:13). I declare Heavenly Father I accept your words as it is written of me. I must continue to be the head and not the tail. I am the first and not the last. I am above all the powers of darkness and not beneath. It is well with me in Jesus' name, Amen.

FAMILY LIFE

Confess three times daily:

FOR EVERYONE

- † **Jesus is Lord** of my life and of my family.

- † **I am prosperous**. I am healthy. My soul prospers in the knowledge of the Lord Jesus, even in Jesus the Word.

- † **Everything I set** my hands to do is successful. I cannot be conquered. I cannot be defeated. I am a stranger to failure. For me to fail God will have to fail; and God cannot fail, therefore, I cannot fail.

- † **The Greater One** indwells me and puts me over. I have His ability. That's what I have, and that's who I am.

- † **No weapon formed** against me shall prosper. Every tongue that accuses me is condemned, for this is my heritage in the Lord and my righteousness is of Him. Amen!

BIBLE REFERENCES for meditation:

3 Jn. 2; Josh. 1:8b; 1 Jn. 4:4; Isa. 54:17

FOR HUSBANDS

✝ **I represent Christ** in this home, so I love my wife (name) even as Christ loved the Church and gave Himself for her.

✝ **Like Jesus, I** cleanse my wife with the washing of water by the Word, that is the word of God coming out of my mouth. I will let no evil communication proceed out of my mouth, and I will not let myself be bitter against her. I will dwell with her in knowledge and wisdom, giving honor unto her as unto the weaker vessel, and as a fellow joint-heir of the grace of life. So our prayers will not be hindered.

> *I represent Christ in this home, so I love my wife (name) even as Christ loved the Church and gave Himself for her.*

✝ **I will always** endeavor to speak to her words of tenderness, kindness, and forgiveness. No man ever hates his own flesh, so I will always nourish and cherish my wife all the days of my life. For she is bone of my bone and flesh of my flesh.

✝ **I will always** put her concern and interest above mine and those of the children. I will frequently bring her presents and flowers, and use tender words like "I love you!," / "Is that my darling!" / "Honey I need you" / "I've really missed you!" /"You're so beautiful!" / "You look great in that dress!" / "I thank God for you!", etc.

✝ **I will not** be moved by any negative thing I see, feel, or hear about her; for I know she is a daughter of God, and she has been put in my care.

✝ **I'll practice Agape,** the God kind of love, with her. As a leader I shall be firm but always fair. I shall be quick to forgive, quick to forget, to repent, and quick to say, "I am sorry, please forgive me darling!"

✝ **I shall be** a good example to my wife and children of what a husband and father should be.

✝ **I will let** no one talk me out of these standards, which are based on the Word of God, and not on traditions of the ungodly.

✝ **When I fall** short of these standards in any way, I shall repent and try again, for 'Quitters Never Win, and Winners Never Quit!' So in my home I'm not a Quitter but a Winner! I can do all things through Christ who strengthens me. Amen!

✝ **I confess that** my wife is humble, submissive, and adaptable to me. She has become my lover, supporter, confidant, prayer-partner, and best friend! God is able, and He is daily working on her. And on me too! We're becoming better lovers, better parents, and better servants of God and of one another. Amen!

BIBLE REFERENCES for meditation:

Eph. 4:29, 5:22, 25-31, 33; Col. 3:19; 1 Pt. 3:7; 2 Cor. 5:7; S.S. 7:1-10; 1 Cor. 13:4-8; 1 Pt. 1:18, 22-25; Ps. 1:1-2; Phil. 4:13; Col. 3:18; Prov. 4:18.

FOR WIVES

✝ **I am the** body of Christ, so I submit to my husband (name) as unto the Lord. I dearly love my husband so I respect, honor, and praise him. I will always support and adapt myself to him.

✝ **I will be** meek, patient, and of a quiet spirit, which is in the sight of God of great price.

✝ **I will try** to please my husband, and satisfy him emotionally and sexually. I'll watch my appearance, my dressing, and my body weight.

✝ **I shall control** my tongue and my thoughts, my actions and reactions.

✝ **I confess that** my husband always cherishes and protects me. He has made me his lover, supporter, confidant, prayer-partner, and best friend.

> I confess that my husband always cherishes and protects me. He has made me his lover, supporter, confidant, prayer-partner, and best friend.

✝ **I have not** received the spirit of fear or of inferiority, but of power, love, and of self-control. I can do all things through Christ who strengthens me. Amen!

✝ **I'll practice Agape (*unconditional love*),** the God kind of love, with him. I'll be a good example to my children, and I'll teach them to respect and obey their parents, especially their father. My husband will come closer to God, because of my godly influence and my constant prayers for him.

✝ **I shall be** a good listener, sympathizer, and confidant of my husband. I shall be quick to forgive, quick to forget, and quick to repent, and to say, "I'm sorry darling, please forgive me!"

✝ **I shall be** like the Virtuous Woman in Proverbs 31. I confess that I am hard working, diligent in my duties as a wife and mother, resourceful in business, disciplined, well mannered, and well-organized, Amen!

✝ **I will let** no one talk me out of these standards, which are based on the Word of God, and not on the traditions of the ungodly.

✝ **When I fall** short of these standards in any way, I shall repent and try again, for 'Quitters Never Win and Winners' Never Quit.' So, in my home, I'm not a Quitter but a Winner! Amen!

✝ **God is able** and He's daily working on my husband, and on me too! We're becoming better lovers, better parents, better servants of God, and of one another. Amen!

BIBLE REFERENCES for meditation:

Eph. 5:22-24; 1 Pt. 3:l-6; S.S. 7:1-10; Prov. 21:9, 19, 23; S.S. 4:7-12; 2 Tim. l:7; Php. 4:13; 1 Pt. 3:l-2; Col. 3:12-14; Prov. 1:10-31; 1 Pt. 1:18, 22-25; Ps. 1:1-2; Prov. 4:18

FOR PARENTS

✝ **Jesus is Lord** of my children (names). They walk in the Spirit, and fulfill not the lusts of the flesh.

✝ **Christ has redeemed** them from all the curses, and like Abraham have been blessed. They're blessed going out and coming in. They're blessed in the morning and in the evening. They're blessed today and everyday of their lives. They're the head and not the tail; the first and not the last. They're above only and never beneath.

✝ **I'll train them** in the way they should go. Rebellion and stubbornness they shall not know.

✝ **I have the** wisdom of God to make my children wise. I'll set no wicked example before their eyes. I will not provoking them to anger, but by the nurture of the Lord, I'll bring them up diligently, taught in the Word.

✝ **Their steps are** ordered and directed each day, for the angels watch and keep them in all their ways. No evil shall befall them, nor sickness bring them low. For I'll teach them to resist it and cause it all to go.

✝ **I'll lift my** hands before them and sing praises to God always, for establishing my seed on earth and fulfilling all their days. Amen!

BIBLE REFERENCES for meditation:

Gal. 5:16; Gal. 3:13-14; Dt. 28:l-14; Tit. 1:6; Eph. 6:4; Ps. 37:23, 91:10-12; Jms. 4:7; Ps. 128

FOR CHILDREN

✝ **I will love** God and obey my parents. I will always honor them, for this is God's commandment with a promise. It shall be well with me and I'll live long on the earth.

I'm growing in grace and in the knowledge of the Lord Jesus.

✝ **I'm growing in** grace and in the knowledge of the Lord Jesus. Like little Jesus, little Moses, and little Samuel, I'm growing daily in wisdom and stature, and in favor with God and with man.

✝ **The angels watch** over me, and Abraham's blessings are mine. Amen!

BIBLE REFERENCES for meditation:

Eph. 6:1-3; 2 Pt. 3:18; Lk. 2:51-52; Mt. 18:10; Ps. 91:11-12; Gal. 3:13-14

FOR RELATIVES AND LOVED ONES

✝ **I confess that** my relatives love God and serve Him. Because I've believed in Jesus, I'm saved and my household. As for me and my house, we shall serve the Lord.

✝ **God does not** desire the death of any sinner, but that all should know Him.

✝ **Therefore, I confess** that Jesus is Lord in the lives of my relatives and loved ones; my parents and in-laws, my brothers and sisters, my uncles and aunties, my nephews and nieces, my grannies, my cousins, my family-dependents, my house-helps, and my family friends (name them).

✝ **I confess that** I love them dearly. I will always forgive any of them who offends me.

✝ **I confess that** they are born-again, baptized in the Holy Spirit, and delivered from all powers of darkness.

✝ **Let them hear** the gospel and be saved. Let them encounter God everywhere they go. Let the angels watch over them and deliver them from any evil they face. Let them be covered with the blood of Jesus. Satan, loosen your grip from any of them, now, and let their needs be met. These I demand in Jesus' Name! Amen!

✝ **I believe their** miracles are happening for God's sake and for my sake. In Jesus' name, Amen!

✝ **My joy is** full, for my loved ones are saved and are serving the Lord. Praise you Father for your mercy and your salvation, Amen.

BIBLE REFERENCES for meditation:

Acts 16:31; Josh. 24:15; 1 Tim. 2:3-6; Zech. l2:12-14; Acts 2:38-39; Col. 1:13; Matt. l9:18-19; Ps. 34:7; Jms. 4:7; Mk. 11:22-26; Jn. l6:23-24

AGAPE POWER

Confess three times daily:

I'm a love child of a love God. The love of God is shed abroad my heart by the Holy Ghost. Therefore I endure long; and I'm patient and kind.

I'm never envious nor boil over with jealousy. I'm not boastful or vainglorious, and I do not display myself haughtily.

Because of God's love, I'm not conceited, or arrogant, or inflated with pride.

I'm neither rude nor unmannerly, and I do not act unbecomingly.

Because of God's love, I do not insist on my own rights or on my own way, for I'm not self-seeking.

I take no account of evil done to me, and I pay no attention to a suffered wrong.

Because of God's love, I do not rejoice at injustice and unrighteousness, but I rejoice when right and truth prevail.

Because of God's love, I bear up under anything and everything that comes.

I'm ever ready to believe the best of every person.

My hopes are fadeless under all circumstances, and I endure all things without weakening.

I can never fail, because love never fails, and never comes to an end.

I'm never moved by what I see or by what I feel. I'm moved only by the Word that's real, the Word of God.

Therefore I call things that be not as though they were.

I always expect a miracle. Something good is going to happen to me this very day. All things work together for my good for I love God and I live as I should.

I rejoice always, pray without ceasing, and in everything give thanks. By so doing I remain in the will of God.

I fight the good fight of Faith. I'm patient in Hope, and I walk in Love.

These are eternal laws of the Kingdom of God. Praise the Lord!

BIBLE REFERENCES for meditation:

Rom. 5:5; 1 Cor. 13:4-8; 2 Cor. 5:7; Rom. 4:17b, 8:28; 1 Thess. 5:16-18; 1 Cor. 13:13; 1 Thess. 1:3

FOR PROVISIONS

JOB, BUSINESS, SCHOOL, EXAM, HOUSING, MONEY, ETC.

I confess that the Lord has given me (specify your need) that I have desired. I ask and it is given to me; I seek and I find; I knock and doors open for me.

My God supplies all my needs, including (list) according to His abundant riches.

God will not withhold any good thing from me. For the earth belongs to the Lord and the fullness thereof, the world and the persons in it. The heart of rulers is in God's hand, and He directs it wherever He wants.

I give generously and God causes me to receive abundantly. Therefore, I confess that I receive good favor everywhere I go.

My desire is granted concerning (list).

Father, release the angels now, to perform for me my stated desires.

Satan, I bind you, hands off my blessings in Jesus' name. I believe I have now received. Thank you Lord. Amen!

BIBLE REFER ENCES for meditation:

Matt. 7:7-9; Phil. 4:19; Ps. 24:l, 84:11; Prov. 21:1; Lk. 6:38; Heb. 1:14; Matt. l8:18-19

STRIFE AND BITTERNESS

Jesus is the Lord in my life, of my thoughts, words and deeds; and even in this situation (specify) Jesus is Lord!

I speak the peace of God into this matter. I reject the spirit of strife and bitterness, in Jesus' name (Galatians 5:25, 26). Amen!

Let the light of God shine within my soul. Let there be love and forgiveness. Let past hurts be healed, and let the future be bright, in Jesus' name. I receive inner healing and the peace of God. Amen!

Let all forces of darkness flee, and let the Spirit of God minister grace. In Jesus' name, Amen!

I refuse to worry and fret about any evil happening around me. Instead I rest in the Lord and wait patiently for Him. So I cease from anger and I forsake all wrath and bitterness.

I confess that I'm tenderhearted, forgiving, slow to speak, and slow to get angry.

I readily forgive those who offend me 70 x 7 times, as Jesus commanded. I pray God's blessing and mercy on them, "Father forgive them, for they know not what they do" (Matthew 18:21).

It is not by power, or by might, but by the Spirit of God. I can do all things through Christ who strengthens me (Zechariah 4:6). Amen!

I, therefore, now release those who have offended me (name them) because I have forgiven them, even as the Lord has forgiven me. Amen!

Lord make me your instrument of peace and love. Thank you Lord for the victory. Praise the Lord! Amen!

BIBLE REFERENCES for meditation:

Gal. 5:25, 26; Ps. 37:7-8; Jms. 1:9; Col. 3:12-13; Matt. 18:21-22; Lk. 6:27-28, 23:34; Zech. 4:6; Php. 4:13; Matt. 18:32-35; 1 Cor. 15:57-58

FEAR, WORRY, DEPRESSION & DOUBT

As a child of God I have not received the spirit of fear, but of power, of love, and of a sound mind (2 Timothy 1:7). I know that the one living in me is greater than the devil in the world.

I dwell in the secret place of the most High, so I abide under the shadow of the Almighty. Truly the Lord is my refuge and my fortress; my God in whom I trust (Psalms 91:1).

A thousand may fall at my side, and ten thousand at my right hand, but it shall not come near me. For He gives His angels charge over me, to keep me in all my ways. They bear me up in their hands lest I dash my foot against a stone (Psalms 91:7, Matthew 4:6).

I call upon the Lord and He answers me and honors me. God is with me in trouble; He delivers me and honors me. With long life He satisfies me, and shows me His salvation. Amen (Psalms 91:16, 103: 2-5)!

Since the Lord is my salvation, whom shall I fear? And since the Lord is the strength of my life, of whom shall I be afraid (Psalms 18:2)?

When the wicked, even my enemies and my foes, come upon me to eat up my flesh, they shall stumble and fall.

Though an host should encamp against me, my heart shall not fear. Though war should rise against me, in this I will be confident (Leviticus. 26:8).

I'm not moved at all by what I see, or by what I feel; I'm moved only by the Word that's real, the Word of God.

I overcome Fear with Faith. Fear is simply, **F**-alse **E**-vidences **A**-ppearing **R**-eal. Faith is **F**-antastic **A**-dventure **I**-n **T**-rusting **H**-im. Amen!

I have also been delivered from the spirit of Worry, for I meditate on the promises, of God, rather than on problems (Philippians 4:6-7).

So by faith I rejoice always. I refuse to be depressed, for the joy of the Lord is my strength (James. 4:7).

I have no anxiety about anything. Instead I pray about everything, and the peace of God which passes all understanding keeps my heart and mind through Christ Jesus (Nehemiah 8:10, Philippians 4:4-7).

I bless the Lord always, and I forget none of His benefits to me; He forgives my sins and heals all my diseases; He delivers me from untimely death, and crowns me with loving kindness and tender mercies; He satisfies my mouth with good things, so that my youth is renewed like the eagle's (Psalms 103:2-5).

I refuse to worry, so God causes others to worry for me. When I pass through the waters of trouble, He is with me; and through the rivers of tribulation, they shall not overflow me; when I walk through the fire of adversity, I shall not be burned (Psalms 103: 2-5).

For He is the Holy One of Israel and my Savior. He gives the heathen and the wicked as a ransom for me, for I am precious in His sight (Isaiah 43:1-4, Proverbs 11:8, 21:18).

God has given me victory over Doubt & Double-mindedness. The saying goes, "Believe & You'll Receive, Doubt & You'll Do Without".

So I confess I believe and I receive; I'm a believer and not a doubter; I doubt my doubts and believe my beliefs (James. 1:5-8)!

So Fear, Worry and Depression I refuse you; be gone in Jesus' name! Doubt, disappear in the name of Jesus! Amen!

I know that all things are now working together for my good, for I love God and I live as I should. Praise the Lord (Romans 8:28)!

BIBLE REFER ENCES for meditation:

2 Tim. 1:7; 1 Jn. 4:4; Ps. 27:1-3, 91; 2 Cor. 5:7; Neh. 8:10; Phil. 4:4-7; Ps. 103: 2-5; Isa. 43:1-4; Prov. 11:8, 21:18; Jms. 1:5-8, 4:7; Mk. 9:23-24; Rom. 8:28

GUILT, INFERIORITY & CONDEMNATION

I am the righteousness of God in Christ; a brand new creation in Him. I can now approach the presence of God with no condemnation of sin.

Because Jesus was made sin for me who knew no sin, that I might be made the righteousness of God in Him (2 Corinthians 5:21).

Therefore no weapon formed against me shall prosper, and every tongue accusing me is condemned; this is my heritage in the Lord and my righteousness is of Him (Isaiah 54:17).

Jesus is my High Priest before the Father, and He is sympathetic and touched by the feeling of my weaknesses. He was in all ways tempted as I am yet without sin.

So I boldly come to God's throne of grace, to obtain mercy, and find grace to help me in time of need (Hebrews 4:14-16).

I daily abstain from all appearance of evil. I daily submit myself to God, in prayer and in His Word; then I resist the devil, and he flees from me (James 4:7).

His Word have I hid in my heart, that I may not sin against Him.

If I fail, I'll run to God and not away from Him. I'll not cover my sins, or make excuse for them; rather I'll confess my sins and forsake them.

Jesus is my Advocate and Defender. He has justified me, so who will separate me from the love of Christ (Romans 8:37- 39)?

I will always forgive those who offend me and I will try to apologize to those I offend.

I'll try to maintain a good conscience before God and before men.

The blood of Jesus continually cleanses me, so I confess that I'm clean in God's sight (Matthew 8:17; 1 Peter 2:24).

Satan cannot accuse me, and men cannot condemn me. Therefore, I reject all spirits of condemnation, fear, and guilt, for His mercy endures forever! Nothing can separate me from God's Love. Amen!

BIBLE REFERENCES for meditation:

2 Cr. 5:17, 21; Isa. 54:17; Heb. 4:14-16; l Thess. 5:22; Matt. 26:41; Jms. 1:7; Prov. 1:13; Jn. 1:8-9, 2:l; Rom. 8:33-35; Matt 8:21-22, 5:23-24; Rom. 12:17-18; 2 Cor. 8:1; 1 Jn. l:7, 3:10; Rv. 12:10b; Rom. 8: 37-38; Ps. 136:1

BLOOD OF JESUS

In the protective power of the blood of Jesus Christ of Nazareth, in the powerful deliverance name of our Lord Jesus Christ of Nazareth, I cover myself with the blood of Jesus Christ. I cover all my relations, my parents, my brothers, my sisters, my wife, my husband, my children, my in-laws, my uncles, my friends and well-wishers with the consecrated blood of our Lord Jesus Christ of Nazareth.

I also cover my house, my business, my office, my properties, my money, my food, my clothes, my vehicles and every other thing that belongs to me with the precious blood of our Lord Jesus Christ of Nazareth in Jesus' name.

I build a hedge of blood around me and all that belongs of relates to me in the mighty name of our Lord Jesus Christ. Amen.

BOLDNESS, POWER, AND FAITH

In the powerful name of our Lord Jesus Christ of Nazareth, Heavenly Father, the Bible says in Proverbs 28:1, "The wicked flee thought no one purses, but the righteous are as bold as a lion."

Father, I ask of your boldness, power and faith to pray this Dangerous Prayer. Let me be bold as a lion and clothe me with your power and faith from on high. It is written in Psalm 62:11, saying God hath spoken once; twice I have heard this that power belongeth unto God.

Heavenly Father, I now receive boldness, power and faith from you in Jesus' Name. I also receive all your weapons of warfare to fight and destroy forever all the plans of Satan and his agents against me. In Jesus' name, Amen.

ANOINTING FOR BATTLE

In the anointed name of our Lord Jesus Christ of Nazareth, Father I lift up my hand towards your heaven. I make a supernatural connection to your throne. Anoint me for battle like you anointed King David in Psalm 89:20-24.

I DECLARE

EVERY DAY, YOU NEED TO DECLARE THE FOLLOWING LOUDLY TO YOURSELF:

†   "I am blessed. I am prosperous. I am successful."

†   "I am victorious. I am talented. I am creative."

†   "I am energetic. I am healthy. I am in shape."

†   "I am energetic. I am happy. I am positive."

†   "I am passionate. I am strong. I am confident."

†   "I am secure. I am beautiful. I am attractive."

†   "I am valuable. I am free. I am redeemed."

†   "I am forgiven. I am anointed. I am accepted."

†   "I am approved. I am prepared. I am qualified."

†   "I am motivated. I am focused. I am disciplined."

†   "I am determined. I am patient. I am kind."

†   "I am generous. I am excellent. I am equipped."

†   "I am empowered. I am well able. I am special."

†   "I am a child of the most High God. I am fearfully and wonderfully made."

WHEN YOU WAKE UP DAILY, LOOK YOURSELF IN THE MIRROR AND DECLARE:

†   I am getting younger. God is renewing my youth like the eagles.

THE ANOINTING BREAKS EVERY YOKE

I declare that God will open the windows of heaven and pour me out a blessing that I will not have room enough to receive it.

Father, thank you for rebuking the devourer for my sake and not allowing him to destroy the fruits of my ground; neither shall my vine cast her fruit before the time in the field.

I rebuke the use of the air waves and news media for satanic purposes and loose them for the propagation of the Gospel of Jesus Christ.

James 5:1-3: Father, I thank Thee that the wealth of the wicked cometh to me now for the building of the Kingdom of God.

I will always remember that:

> Whether the devil likes it or not, I will always act like I am blessed, talk like I am blessed, walk like I am blessed, think like I am blessed, smile like I am blessed, and dress like I am blessed!

† I am the anointed one!

† I am the creative one!

† I am the talented one!

† I am the successful one!

† I have the favor of God around me!

† People like me everywhere I go!

† I remain a victor and not a victim, above only and not beneath!

I declare and decree that I am blessed. Whether the devil likes it or not, I will always act like I am blessed, talk like I am blessed, walk like I am blessed, think like I am blessed, smile like I am blessed, and dress like I am blessed. I will always put positive actions around my faith, and soon I will see it become a reality.

I declare that I will not suffer years of sorrow; I will not suffer years of shame. I will not suffer years of slavery. I will not suffer years of defeat. I command every spirit of delay of progress in my life to be destroyed by fire, in Jesus' Name, Amen. I will live in victory. I will be a victor and not a victim.

I will be decisive. I will be steadfast. I will be God honoring. I will be honest. I will be holy. I will never be depressed. I rebuke every adversity in my life to be consumed by fire. I will pass every test set for me by God. I will not worry. I will not be discouraged. I will continue to experience total wholeness, spirit, soul and body. God will bring me to a new position of promotion and breakthrough.

I declare that I have complete wholeness and total healing of my body from any type of sickness or disease. God will heal my wounds, my hurts and every scar in my body, soul and spirit and God will bring me into a new level of victory and power. Every hurt and wound from my past or present is healed completely, IN JESUS' NAME, Amen.

I declare and decree that God open a great door of prosperity for me and that God destroy all my enemies and adversaries. I pray for an out pouring of the Holy Spirit and for God to prepare and equip me for His work. I declare and decree that anger, self-pity, bitterness, resentment, withdrawal, revenge and unforgiveness in me will be gone, in the name of Jesus!

I declare that God will strengthen the leaders in authority and raise new leaders who are full of the power and anointing of God. I pray that all leaders in authority will lead with the fear of God.

I bind every deceitful and lying spirit, spirit of fear, and doubt that have built strongholds around me. I pray for God's protection to be upon me and every member of my family. I declare continued progress and success over my life. God will restore my health and heal me of every sickness (Jeremiah 30:17). I command my spirit and body to be supernaturally empowered and charged by God's power for breakthrough and success.

I declare that I will draw daily from God's immeasurable, inexhaustible supply of strength, grace and mercy. By God's spirit within me, I am equipped to walk daily in God's *dunamis* power. I command every bitterness and indignation and wrath (passion, rage, bad temper) and resentment (anger, animosity,) and quarreling (brawling, clamor, contention) and slander (evil speaking, abusive or blasphemous language) be banished from me, with all malice (spite, ill-will or wickedness of any kind). I get rid of all anger, IN JESUS' NAME, Amen.

I declare by God's spirit living within me, I am supernaturally empowered and can draw upon the peace of God that passes human understanding. I have inexhaustible supply of God's strength, His love, His mercy, His power! Though my outward man, my physical body is subject to weakness and decay, my spirit is renewed day by day. So I will not faint, regardless of what comes my way, I will never be defeated, I will never give up. By God's Spirit within me, I am equipped and prepared to walk in might, power and victory on a daily basis.

> I have presented my body as a living sacrifice to God and my members as weapons of righteousness for His daily use.

I declare and decree that I will not feel empty, dry, weary, and overwhelmed by any circumstances I am facing. I will do whatever is necessary to shut myself in with God to see me through. I will get alone with my God and draw strength from Him. I will discipline myself where I am on a daily basis drawing upon His grace and power to breakthrough.

I choose to be a victor, not a victim. I turn my hurts and wounds into victories and do not allow them to torment me. I determine by an act of my will to refuse to become offended when persecuted or at times of adversity (Romans 12:14-17), but will bless and pray that I live long enough to prosper to the shame and disappointment of my enemies. I will make every effort as far as possible to live peaceably with people (Romans 12:18-21; 1 Peter 3:8-9). I will crucify my flesh and cannot feel any attacks. I will live in the spirit. None of the attacks on me will move me. I am unmovable and will overcome any obstacle, IN JESUS' NAME, Amen.

I will live today in full, I will forget the past. **I will not worry about tomorrow. Jesus Christ lives in me. I cannot fail. For me to fail, God will have to fail, and because my God cannot fail, I cannot fail.** As a child of God, I have been redeemed from all sin. I have been forgiven, cleansed and empowered by the Holy Spirit to live in victory. I have unmerited favor and all spiritual blessing that I need to prosper and serve God in peace.

I declare that in all circumstances, God will be in control and will be directing my steps and working out His miracle in my life.

I declare that I am meditating the scripture day and night. I picture myself dead to the power and appeal of sin. I have removed every provision for sinful habits. I have cleansed my heart and mind of impure imaginations. I am accountable to God-given authority. I am obeying the promptings of God's Spirit. I fast to increase my alertness to God's promptings. I have presented my body as a living sacrifice to God and my members as weapons of righteousness for His daily use.

Heavenly Father, I ask You in the name and through the blood of the Lord Jesus Christ to bind and rebuke Satan and put a hedge of protection around me and each one in my family, "being confident of this very thing, that he which hath begun a good work in me will perform it until the day of Jesus Christ" (Philippians 1:6).

GOD'S COVENANT ANOINTING

Covenant Deed: "The deed constituting the evidence of a person's legal ownership." (Webster's Dictionary)

"'The days are coming,' declares the LORD, 'when I will make a new covenant with the people of Israel and with the people of Judah. It will not be like the covenants I made with their ancestors when I took them by the hand to lead them out of Egypt because they broke my covenant, though I was a husband to them', declares the LORD. 'This is my covenant I will make the people of Israel after that time,' declares the lord. 'I will put my law in their minds and write it on their hearts. I will be their God and they will be my people'" (Jeremiah 31:31-33).

As Abraham's seed you have inherited ALL the promises made to Israel under the Old Covenant (Galatians 3:16, 29) and even greater promises under the New Covenant. All of God's promises are confirmed and fulfilled through Christ (2 Corinthians 1:20) and have been forever sealed and put into effect with the ALL POWERFUL blood of Jesus!

Listed below are some of the covenant promises that belong to you NOW. Take hold of these and appropriate them daily to your life. As God's spiritual Israel, God has given **You** these covenant promises as part of our inheritance:

† I am a "peculiar treasure," God's prized possession (Exodus 19:5).

† I am a king and priest upon this earth (Revelation 5:9-11).

† I am a "holy nation" (1 Peter 2:9-10).

† God will be an enemy to my enemies (Exodus 23:22).

† God will bless my daily provisions (Exodus 23:25).

† God will take sickness from me (Exodus 23:25).

† God will prolong my days upon the earth (Deuteronomy 4:40).

† God will drive out my enemies from before us (Deuteronomy 4:37-38).

† God will love, bless, and multiply me (Deuteronomy 7:13).

† God will bless me above the nations of the earth (Deuteronomy 28:1).

† God will bless me wherever I am in the city or the country (Deuteronomy 28:3).

† God's blessing will be upon my children (Deuteronomy 28:4).

† God's blessing will be upon my income and all my efforts (Deuteronomy 28:8).

> God will command His blessing to be upon me in all that I undertake.

† God will continually increase my supply (Deuteronomy 28:11).

† God will command His blessing to be upon me in all that I undertake (Deuteronomy 28:8).

† I will abound in prosperity, in goods, in children, and in crops in all the land (Deuteronomy 28:11).

† God will open up His storehouse. He will become my total supply (Deuteronomy 28:12).

† God will bless all the work of my hands (Deuteronomy 28:12).

† God will prosper me enough to lend and I will not need to borrow (Deuteronomy 28:120).

† God will make ME the head and not the tail; I will be above, not underneath (Deuteronomy 28:13).

Under the New Covenant, as joint-heirs of the Kingdom of God, you have also inherited the following covenant promises:

† God has redeemed me and cleansed me from all sin (Galatians 3:13).

† I have been set free from the power of sin (Romans 6:18).

† I have eternal life (1 John 5:13).

† I have been granted access into the Holy of Holies to meet with God (Ephesians 2:13-14).

† God has made me His child and has placed His Spirit within me (Luke 10:19).

† Through the Holy Spirit I have been given power over all the power of the enemy (Luke 10:19).

† Through the Holy Spirit I have been given the "dynamic" miracle-working power of God (Acts 1:8).

† I have been given the gifts of the Spirit (1 Corinthians 12:7-11).

† Through the Holy Spirit the fruit of the Spirit is manifested in my life (Galatians 5:22-23).

† I have been given power and authority in the Name of Jesus (Mark 16:17-18).

† I can ask anything in the Name of Jesus and it will be done (John 14:13-14).

† I am being conformed into the image of Christ by the Spirit working in me (Romans 8:29).

† I am an overcomer on this earth through the blood of Jesus (Revelation 12:11).

✝ I will one day have a glorified body (1 Corinthians 15:50-53).

✝ I will be gathered together to meet Christ at His coming (1 Thessalonians 4:15-17).

✝ I will rule and reign with Christ for a thousand years (Revelation 20:4).

✝ I will see God face-to-face and live forever in the promised land—the New Jerusalem—He has prepared for us (Revelation 21:2-3).

BREAKING THE CYCLE OF FAILURE:

UNDERTSANDING THE WORD FAILURE

WEBSTER'S DICTIONARY defines the word failure very clearly: "*To be or become deficient or lacking, to stop functioning or operating, to break, bend or be otherwise destroyed, or be made useless.*"

Moreover, Vine's Bible Dictionary credits the word fail to Greek origins, and proclaims that it comes from the word *Apopsucho*, literally meaning "*to lose breath of faint in heart, or something attacking your emotional heart.*"

Luke 21:26: "People will faint from terror, apprehensive of what is coming on the world, for heavenly bodies will be shaken."

POINT ONE

- † There is a difference in Failing and becoming a Failure.

- † Failing is common to all Men and Women.

- † Because you failed in an area of life does not make you a failure.

- † Only your believing you are a failure makes you a failure.

- † Therefore, to change your life you must change your belief system.

- † Many have made their failures their "Point of Reference" for the rest of their lives.

- † You must have a new confession come from your mouth, "I have failed now and in the past, but I'm not a failure."

POINT 2

Remember the cycle of failure is being defeated in the same area, again and again.

For example:

       ✝ Sickness that can be caused by a spirit of Affliction.

       ✝ Addiction

       ✝ Perversion

       ✝ Financial Struggles

       ✝ Relationship Struggles

       ✝ Divorce

       ✝ Living for God

       ✝ Fear of Witchcraft

> The cycle of failure is being defeated in my life, again and again.

POINT 3

Three main things that will try to make you believe that you are a failure.

       ✝ Hereditary

       ✝ Your programming

       ✝ Familiar Spirits

HEREDITARY

Hereditary can be the passing or capability of passing naturally from parent to offspring through the genes. In other words being transmitted from one to another.

Doctors believe sickness can live in a family line.

The Bible teaches that weakness can be passed down a family line or by Familiar Spirits. The Bible calls it **INIQUITY**.

The word "INIQUITY" means: "to bend or to <u>distort the heart</u>" (Webster's Dictionary). It also implies <u>a certain weakness or predisposition toward a certain sin.</u>

<u>Note</u>: If a sin is repeatedly committed, it becomes an **INIQUITY** which can be passed down through the bloodline. The failure becomes part of the family. Many times the offspring of said family will have a weakness for the same kind of Sin.

Here are some examples:

✝ Homosexuals

✝ Alcoholism

✝ Mental Illness

✝ Drug Addictions

An iniquity is more than just a sin. An iniquity is our ancestors' battle or weakness, which has become our struggle.

But the Good News is that by the "Power of Jesus Christ and his shed Blood on Calvary" the iniquity or weakness can stop with you and not be passed on to the next generation.

<u>Exodus 20:5</u>: "You shall not bow down to them or worship them; for I, the LORD your God, am a jealous God, punishing the children for the sin of the parents to the third and fourth generation of those who hate me."

<u>Note</u>: **If a family is not cleansed of iniquity, then each generation becomes worse than the last.**

✝ We must, **B-R-E-A-K** generational curses by the **<u>Blood of Jesus Christ.</u>**

Revelation 1:5: "[A]nd from Jesus Christ, who is the faithful witness, the firstborn from the dead, and the ruler of the kings of the earth. To him who loves us and has freed us from our sins by his blood."

Acts 16:31: "They replied, 'Believe in the Lord Jesus, and you and your household will be saved.'"

Jesus will wash you and your household in His Blood.

Romans 10:9: "If you declare with your mouth 'Jesus is Lord' and believe in your heart that God raised Him from the dead, you will be saved."

The word "saved," has a Greek equivalent, *sozo*.

It means:

- † Deliverance from danger;

- † Deliverance from the bondage of sin;

- † Kept from sickness, and from failing.

POINT 4

SHAME

THE POWER OF YOUR SECRETS

The word SHAME means: "A painful emotion caused by consciousness of guilt" (Webster's Dictionary).

Note: Guilt can be real or false, and both have the same power to rob you of life.

Those living with Shame must constantly attempt to cope with the painful "SECRETS."

Shame gives place to FEAR, and allows it to intertwine with WORRY. You will begin to give place to thoughts such as, "What if they find out my secret sins, then I will really be in trouble!"

This frightful thought opens the door for control by evil spirits.

The Original Source of SHAME

Gen 3:10: "And he [Adam] answered, 'I heard you in the garden, and I was afraid because I naked; so I hid.'"

DO NOT HIDE FROM THE LIGHT

John 3:21:"But whoever lives by the truth comes into the light, so that it may be seen plainly that what they have done has been done in the sight of God."

POINT 5

REPROGRAMING YOUR MIND

Romans 12:1-2

For this reason I make request to you, brothers, by the mercies of God, that you will give your bodies as a living offering, holy, pleasing to God, which is the worship it is right for you to give him.

And let not your behavior be like that of this world, **but be changed and made new in mind**, so that by experience you may have knowledge of the good and pleasing and complete purpose of God.

These fifteen truths should be confessed daily to build the believer's self-esteem.

It is critical for the believer to see himself as God looks at him. John the Baptist saw himself and spoke in agreement with the way God saw him.

The discipline to speak God's Word will transform your thinking; it will change how you see yourself and your level of Faith will soar.

As you see yourself differently, you will respond to others differently.

Always remember, there are two truths: What man or circumstances say and what God says. Choose to believe God because your circumstance is only temporary.

1. **2 Corinthians 5:17**

    † I am a New Creature predestined for greatness.

2. **John 1:12**

    † I am a Child of God fully accepted by the Father.

3. **Romans 5:8**

    † I am loved by God regardless of how I perform.

4. **1 John 1:9**

   † I am forgiven and will not be tormented by my past errors.

5. **1 John 5:4**

   † I am an overcomer and my faith is changing my circumstances.

6. **2 Corinthians 9:8**

   † I am a giver and God is causing people to help me prosper.

7. **Luke 10:17**

   † I have authority over the devil and no demon power can hurt me.

8. **John 10:10**

   † Abundance is God's will for me and I will not settle for less.

9. **1 Peter 2:24**

   † I am healed and sickness will not lord over my body.

10. **Psalm 118:6**

    † God is on my side; I will not fear.

11. **Philippians 4:7**

    † The Holy Spirit is my helper; I'm never alone and I have the peace of God.

12. **Ephesians 1:3 and 2 Corinthians 4:18**

    † I am blessed and it's a matter of time before things change. What I see now is only temporary.

13. 1 Corinthians 1:30

✝ I have the wisdom of God; I hear the Father's voice; my steps are ordered by God and the voice of a stranger I will not follow.

14. Corinthians 12:20-25 and Ephesians 4:11-12

✝ I am set in the body of Christ and I know that I am valuable and important to the work of God.

15. Matthew 5:1-12

✝ I choose not to be offended, and I am being delivered out of all afflictions and persecutions.

POINT 7

Man is made up of three (3) parts: Body, Soul and Spirit. He is a spirit being, living in a physical body and possessing a soul.

When a person is having a drug challenge and comes to the Lord for salvation, his spirit becomes alive to God. His flesh (body) has been trained to misbehave and sin.

So, now, the person has to take the Word of God, feed his spirit, renew his mind in order to overcome his flesh (body), and glorify God with his life.

THE FORTY (40) I AM'S

Confessing the Forty (40) I am(s) on a daily basis will cause you to see yourself the way God sees you.

The opinions of others don't offend you when you know who you are. In Christ you are:

1. I am a Child of God—Romans 8:16;

2. I am redeemed from the Hand of the Enemy—Psalms 107:2;

3. I am forgiven—Colossians 1:13-14;

4. I am saved by Grace through Faith—Ephesians 2:8;

5. I am justified—Romans 5:1;

6. I am sanctified—1 Corinthians 1:2;

7. I am a new Creature—2 Corinthians 5:17;

8. I am a partaker of His Divine Nature—2 Peter 1:4;

9. I am redeemed from the Curse of the Law—Galatians 3:13;

10. I am delivered from the Powers of Darkness—Colossians 1:13;

11. I am led by the Spirit of God—Romans 8:14;

12. I am a son of God—Romans 8:14;

13. I am kept in Safety wherever I go—Psalm 91:11;

14. I am getting all My needs Met by Jesus—Philippians 4:19;

15. I am casting All My Cares on Jesus—1 Peter 5:7;

16. I am strong in the Lord and in the Power of His Might—Ephesians 6:10;

17. I am doing All things through Christ who Strengthens Me—Philippians 4:13;

18. I am an heir of God and a Joint heir with Jesus—Romans 8:17;

19. I am Heir to the Blessing of Abraham—Galatians 3:13-14;

20. I am Observing/Doing the Lord's Commandments—Deuteronomy 28:12;

21. I am Blessed Coming in and Blessed Going out—Deuteronomy 28:6;

22. I am an heir of Eternal life—1 John 5:11-12;

23. I am blessed with all Spiritual Blessing—Ephesians 1:3;

24. I am healed by His Stripes—1 Peter 2:24;

25. I am exercising My Authority over the Enemy—Luke 10:19;

26. I am above only and not beneath—Deuteronomy 28:13;

27. I am more than a Conqueror—Romans 8:37;

28. I am establishing God's word here on Earth—Matthew 16:19;

29. I am an over-comer by the Blood of the Lamb and the Word of my Testimony—Revelation 12:11;

30. I am daily overcoming the Devil—1 John 4:4;

31. I am not moved by what I see—2 Corinthians 4:18;

32. I am walking by Faith and Not by Sight—2 Corinthians 5:7;

33. I am casting Down Vain Imaginations—2 Corinthians 10:4-5;

34. I am bringing Every Thought into Captivity—2 Corinthians10:5;

35. I am being transformed by renewing my mind—Romans 12:1-2;

36. I am a laborer together with God—1 Corinthians 3:9;

37. I am the Righteousness of God in Christ—2 Corinthians 5:21;

38. I am an Imitator of Jesus—Ephesians 5:1;

39. I am the light of the World—Matthew 5:14;

40. I am blessing the Lord at all times and continually praising the Lord with My mouth—Psalm 34:1.

POINT 8

GENERAL INTERCESSORY PRAYER AND FAITH CONFESSION

Here is a general intercessory prayer that the family member or significant other can use when their loved one is challenged with an addiction.

When a person is in the grip of an addiction, they are being attacked in their soulish realm.

Therefore, they may want to stop using and receive help, but the satanic forces that are influencing them have them "spiritually blinded."

This form of intercessory prayer is effective in allowing the person to be loosed from the devil's influence, so that they can make a Godly decision to come to Christ.

It should be prayed in Faith and then confessed with thanksgiving to God until the person's deliverance manifests.

Prayer:

Father, in the name of Jesus, I hold up _____ before you. I pray and confess your word over him/her and as I do; I believe that your perfect will is being done in his life. Father, I bind the satanic forces around him and I cast them out with your Word.

I take authority over the powers of witchcraft so that _____ can be free to receive from you. Father, as I stand in the gap and intercede on his behalf.

I believe that you are arranging the perfect witness to cross his path to share the gospel with him in a way that he will listen and understand it. Father, you promise to deliver those for whom we intercede. So, based on your word, I thank you for _____.

Deliverance and salvation. And now Father, I cast the whole of my care upon you; therefore, I believe that my faith is changing the situation. In Jesus' name, Amen!

BREAKING THE CYCLE OF FAILURE DECLARATION

Thank you, Lord, for investing in Your servant the right to be cleansed from all Sin and its affect on my life and the life of my children.

We receive by Faith in Jesus Christ the complete cleansing of our sins _____, and cleansing from all unrighteousness. We appropriate the power of the Cross and the shed Blood of Jesus to stop all judgments and curses affecting my life from my sin and the sins of my family line (1 John 1:9).

We bind you, Satan, you and your army, and we refuse you any right to carry out any curses against _____.

We break the sowing and reaping cycle that was set up by the ancestral sins and curses, and we speak death to all evil seeds that were sown, on the authority of the Name of Jesus and His finished work on the Cross.

We declare that Christ redeemed me from the curse of the law by becoming a curse for me so that by faith I will receive the promises of God. Lord, whom you set free is free indeed.

Thank you Lord that _____ is in a new family where there are no Sins of the fathers and thus no Resulting Curses. In the Name of Jesus Christ we pray. Amen!

FORGIVENESS PRAYERS

FORGIVING OTHERS

Father, You have made it clear that you desire the healing and freedom for me that forgiveness brings.

You require that I forgive so I can receive Your forgiveness. Therefore, I choose to forgive _____ for _____.

In the excellent name of our Lord Jesus Christ of Nazareth, Father I forgive all the people who have sinned against me through thoughts, words and action. I forgive all who have set me up to enter into sin and all who have hurt me out of their own hurts.

I forgive all of them with all of my heart, my soul and my mind. Father, forgive me all my sins for I have forgiven every one that has sinned against me. Lead me not into temptation and do not allow me to enter into temptation by myself. In Jesus' name, Amen (Mark 11:25-26; Luke 11:4).

I release them from any debt that I thought they owed me. I let go of all judgments and punishments that I have wanted them to have.

I turn all of this and them over to you. In the Name of Jesus I pray. Amen!

ASKING GOD'S FORGIVENESS

Father, now that I have forgiven all others, I come to you through the shed blood of Jesus and the power of His Cross and ask You to forgive me for all my sins.

I acknowledge and take responsibility for each and every time I have violated Your commandments as well as for the sinful thoughts and plans that have been and are in my heart.

Holy Spirit, I thank You for working forgiveness into my life, for healing me, and for cleansing me from all unrighteousness.

Thank you, Father, for restoring me to fellowship with You in the name of Jesus Christ. Amen!

FORGIVING MYSELF

In the merciful name of our Lord Jesus Christ of Nazareth, Heavenly Father, in any way I have sinned against myself, through thoughts, words and actions, I forgive myself in Jesus' name. I repent of every sin against myself and I destroy all the hindrances of sin against me. I cancel all the works of darkness against me through sin (1 Corinthians 6:18-20).

Father, because You have forgiven me, I choose to forgive myself for all the ways I have hurt others out of my own hurts, and the ways I have hurt myself.

> I choose to forgive and release myself for all accusations, judgments, hatred, and slander I have made against myself.

I choose to forgive and release myself for all accusations, judgments, hatred, and slander I have made against myself. I forgive myself for the mistakes, stupidity, and other ways I have fallen short of the mark.

I choose to accept myself just as I am at this time, because I know that you, Lord, accept me just the way that I am.

I know that You love me. So I choose to begin to love myself. And yet I know that you will not leave me in this condition, but you will draw me onward, freeing me from my current state.

Holy Spirit, I give you permission to work Your work of sanctification in me. I embrace fully, and look forward to, your changing me into the image of Christ. In the Name of Jesus Christ I pray. Amen!

SEXUAL HEALING CONFESSION

If you're battling in the area of sexual sins here is a confession that will help you to reprogram your mind. Confessed this seven times a day out loud:

Father, in the Name of Jesus, I submit myself completely to you. I confess all of my emotional and sexual sins, as well as my ungodly soul ties. I choose to forgive each person that I have been involved with in any ungodly way. I ask You, Lord, to forgive me for my sin that resulted in ungodly ties.

Lord, I receive your forgiveness. Thank You for forgiving me, and for cleansing me. I choose to forgive myself to no longer be angry at myself, hate myself, or punish myself. Lord, I break my ungodly soul ties with.

I release myself from him/her, and I release him/her from me. As I do this, Lord, I pray that You would cause him/her to be all that You want him/her to be, and that You would cause me to be all that You want me to be.

Lord, please cleanse my mind from all memories of ungodly unions, so I am totally free to give myself to You and to my mate.

I renounce and cancel the assignments of all evil spirits attempting to maintain these ungodly memories.

Lord, thank you for restoring my soul to wholeness. Let me walk in holiness by Your grace. In the Name of Jesus Christ I pray.

Lord Jesus Christ I ask for Your ability to live an clean life by the power of your word and Holy Spirit. Amen.

A SINNER'S PRAYER TO BE BORN AGAIN

Heavenly Father, I come to You in the name of Jesus. I know that I am lost and cannot save myself. Thank You for loving me and for sending your only begotten Son to die for my sins. In obedience to Your Word, I now confess with my mouth that Jesus is my Lord and Savior, and He's the Master of my life. I believe that God raised Him from the dead. I believe He has taken my sins away by His blood, and He has reconciled me to God. I now receive the gift of eternal life. I am now bound for Heaven and not Hell. Thank You for making me a child of God, and for giving me the righteousness of Christ. Amen!

Bible Passages: Eph. 2:8-10; Rom. 3:23; Jn. 3:16; Rom. 10:9-10, 13; 2 Cor. 5:17, 21; 1 Jn. 5:13.

ABOUT THE AUTHOR

Bright Osigwe is a Pastor, Chaplain, International Bible conference teacher and motivational speaker, with uncommon wealth of experiences and personal insights on how to achieve a victorious living. He is the President of New Heart Assembly Ministries (Bright Compassion Center), which is committed to helping the poor and needy, distributing free Bibles and Christian literature, and church planting. His ministry has supported many Widows and Orphans, and is based on "Passion for God, and Compassion for People." Rev. Bright Osigwe has taught and proclaimed the gospel with signs and wonders in Africa, Asia, Europe, South America, Central America, the Middle East and North America.

Pastor Bright Osigwe

Printed in the United States
By Bookmasters